THIRTY D

MW00378594

Sam and Ann Phillips

Thirty Days of Round Pen Training

(For Horses and For Life)

Short devotions for lovers of horses, Both young and old

Sam and Ann Phillips

Acknowledgements

I would like to recognize my Mom and Dad for their contribution to my love of horses and being my first teachers. They bought my first horse.

Much thanks to Skipper Calder of Cowboy-Up Ministry for his Sunday after Sunday of teaching horse training and ministry of God's word.

I would like to give credit to Paul Daily of Wild Horse Ministries who gave inspiration and confirmation of this book.

To my wife who thought I should and could write this devotional book, together we have finished it. Without her, it would not have been possible.

Special thanks to all the horses who have tolerated all the things I did wrong while learning a better way of training.

Sam and Ann Phillips

Dedication

For all the young people and adults that have love for horses and for Christ. How you work with your horse is very much like the way the Lord will work with you. We're made for God's enjoyment and for His Service, just as the horse was made for people's enjoyment and for service.

Sam and Ann Phillips

Forward

Horses are large animals. The way of a horse in the wild is to protect themselves. It is much the same when they live in your barn and are owned by you. They have fears that are a part of who they are. In the wild, animals may attack them. Their defense is to flee or fight. Until they learn to trust their owner, you are just another animal. Your job is to teach them to trust you. When they do, they will be a great friend and a wonderful ride. But be very careful, otherwise you could be harmed. Always have an adult with you if you are young. If you are teenager, this may not be necessary but continue to remember that safety is important. Horses, even tame ones, can spook at an unusual site or sound. Be alert and ready to calm the horse and protect yourself.

NOTE: Scriptures are from the NIrV unless otherwise indicated.

Sam and Ann Phillips

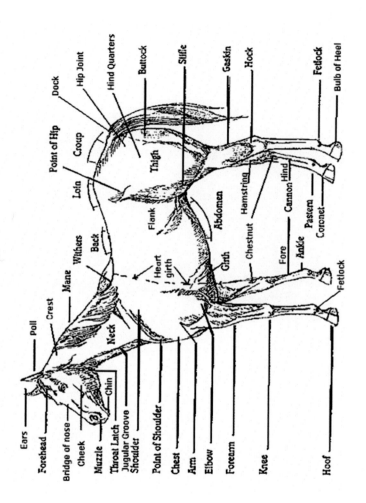

Knowing the parts of your horse

• Chosen for training
• Chosen for the Master's use

DAY 1

HORSE LESSON:

Some horses, when they are chosen, are not very pretty and their actions are unpredictable. They may be out of shape, and either underweight or overweight. Some have physical problems and attitude problems, but with the master's care and training, they can become what the master wants them to be. No matter what size, shape, or temperament, there is a purpose for every horse and every person.

LIFE LESSON

Submit to training and become all that God wants you to be. God has chosen YOU. He chose the color of the sky, color of the grass, and color of horses. It is not important for you to be like others, because He made you special and one of a kind. Every day, God is training you for that plan He has for your life. Listen closely and find out what lesson He wants you to learn.

What challenges have I had today that God might be trying to teach me that will help me in my future?

Jeremiah 29:11 - "I know the plans I have for you," announces the LORD. "I want you to enjoy success. I do not plan to harm you. I will give you hope for the years to come."

John 15:16 - You did not choose me. Instead, I chose you. I appointed you so that you might go and bear fruit that will last. I also appointed you so that the Father will give you what you ask for. He will give you whatever you ask for in my name.

DAY 2

- Finding relief

HORSE LESSON:
A horse seeks relief from pressure. A wise trainer knows to relieve pressure at the first response when a horse yields to his or her instruction. When you pull the reins, it puts pressure on the horse's mouth. When he moves to the pressure, the pressure is relieved. How do you handle pressure? Sometimes, you may explode and fight against the pressure, or you may try to run away from it. But that only makes the pressure greater. Yielding to the pressure of a good master brings relief.

Good hands make a soft mouth. That means that if you stop the pressure when the horse reacts correctly, he will begin to obey you quickly.

LIFE LESSON

Our response to God's word brings relief from guilt and release from punishment. Through training, we learn to respond quickly to the commandment of God and His reward always follows. Christ is a Good Master. What challenges have I had today that God might be trying to teach a lesson that will help me in my future?

Matthew 11:28 "Come to me, all you who are tired and are carrying heavy loads. I will give you rest.

Psalms 8"6:11 LORD, teach me how you want me to live.

Do this so that I will depend on you, my faithful God.

Give me a heart that doesn't want anything
more than to worship you.

Matthew 19:16 Just then, a man came up to Jesus. He asked, "Teacher, what good thing must I do to receive eternal life?"

17 "Why do you ask me about what is good?" Jesus replied. "There is only one who is good. If you want to enter the kingdom, obey the commandments."

DAY 3

- Learning to trust

HORSE LESSON:

Does your horse stand still while you approach him? Or does he move away? It is only natural for a horse to move away from things that he is unsure of. Trust is developed by teaching the horse that you will not harm him. With time and experience, the horse will learn that he can depend on your leadership to get him out of troublesome situations. Without trust, training will be very difficult.

In the round pen, when your horse stands for you to approach, and then follows when you walk away, you will know that he is beginning to trust your leadership. Trust is the foundation for the relationship between you and your horse. Trust cannot be forced. It is earned. We must be trustworthy.

LIFE LESSON:

Like the horse, we need to learn to trust God and His leadership to become all that He wants us to be.

God is dependable. He is waiting for us to follow Him and show that we trust Him. He wants us to be reliable also. He wants to be able to trust us and desires that others can depend upon us too.

What challenges have I had today that God might be trying to teach a lesson that will help me in my future? Have others learned that you are dependable? Write your thoughts about trust.

Hebrews 11: 6 Without faith, it is impossible to please God. Those who come to God must believe that he exists. And they must believe that he rewards those who look to him.

Proverbs 3: 5 Trust in the LORD with all your heart. Do not depend on your own understanding. 6 In all your ways obey him. Then he will make your paths smooth and straight.

DAY 4

Discipline
- There needs to be respect
- Correction is necessary

HORSE LESSON:
If your horse is to respect you, you must correct him within three seconds for unacceptable behavior every time. You must be consistent. Reward right behavior equally as quick with an approving word or touch. Make right things easy and wrong things difficult. Be gentle and kind, but be firm.

Respect is the appropriate response to pressure.

LIFE LESSON:

Your horse will learn the correct response by your approval and reward. He will also learn what is unacceptable from your correction. You are the leader. We all make wrong choices. We do wrong things just like the horse does wrong things. Training is about learning what is right and making right choices. Parents and/or leaders are training you to make right choices. They must correct wrong behavior. You can soon be making good choices for your life.

What are lessons I have learned about making good choices?

_____   _____

_____

_____

_____

What choices have I made that need correction and in what ways do I need to learn to make better choices?

Proverbs 3:6   In all your ways remember him. Then He will make your paths smooth and straight.

> *Proverbs 1:7* If you really want to gain knowledge, you must begin by having respect for the LORD.
>   But foolish people hate wisdom and instruction.
>
> *James 4:6* But God continues to give us more grace. That's why Scripture says,
>
> "God opposes those who are proud.
>   But he gives grace to those who are humble."

DAY 5

- Pay attention

HORSE LESSON:
In order to train your horse, you must have his full attention. He must be listening to you and waiting for your cues of what you want from him. There are many distracting sights and sounds that draw his focus from you. When he is paying attention to them, he is not focused on you. Grass can be a distraction, and he wants to eat instead of train. That is why you see round pens where a horse is trained with no grass. Dogs, people, machinery, wind, water...things that not only distract but sometimes frighten. Not giving his full attention is disrespectful, and you must give correction to get his attention.

Make training enjoyable for the horse and learn the length of his attention span. Stop on a success of obedience. Help your horse make your idea "his idea".

LIFE LESSON:

It is disrespectful to not give God our full attention. Life is much easier when we follow God's plan for our lives…when we listen closely to His words and obey.

Do you give your parents and/or leaders your full attention so you will learn the lessons of life that is important for you to know?

What things are distracting you from listening to training in your life? Is it friends? What else?

_____   _____
_____   _____
_____   _____
_____   _____

I Peter 5:8 Be watchful and control yourselves. Your enemy the devil is like a roaring lion. He prowls around looking for someone to swallow up.

Jeremiah 29:13 When you look for me with all your heart, you will find me.

DAY 6

- Lunging a Horse
- Teaching direction

HORSE LESSION:

Lunging a horse is when you are standing in the middle of a round pen and your horse at the end of a long rope going in one direction and then the other. To lunge your horse, you take the rope in one hand and point in the direction you want him to go. You put pressure on him to move with a rope or crop as you point with the other hand.

When you want to stop the horse from lunging, pull his head in and look at his hips. He should stop and look at you. Then, you should look away and take the pressure off. Let him rest and be rewarded for responding correctly. He should not come to you until you ask.

LIFE LESSON:

This is the way that God moves us. He points the direction we should go with His hand, either by a Bible scripture or talking to your heart. He applies pressure with the other hand and keeps us mindful that He is in control. If you, a horse person, control the speed and direction of your horse, you are truly in control.

The training from God is always for your good. He only has good thoughts toward you, and He wants the best for your life.

God loves you and knows you by name. Each lesson you learn as He directs you will build upon the next lesson. Your obedience will cause you to grow in your knowledge of Him and what He wants you to do.

What direction is God pointing you today? Could it be to speak a kind word to someone that is sad and needs a friend? Perhaps it is to be bold about your faith in Him. Look into His Word and listen for His voice. Write your thoughts about this lesson.

_____

_____

_____

_____

_____

_____

_____

Psalms 119:105 Your word is like a lamp that shows me the way. It is like a light that guides me.

DAY 7

- Does your horse lead?
- Where are your steps leading you?

HORSE LESSON

Does your horse lead? Or, is your horse leading you? You must be the one in control-telling the horse where to go, when, and how fast. First, you take the lead rope in your hand and the remainder of the rope in your other hand. You face the direction that you want to go and pull pressure on the lead. When your horse steps forward, stop and reward him for following. Repeat the step over and over until your horse is following your lead. You decide the distance that you want your horse to be from you. To stop your horse from walking, you stop and then pull on the lead in a downward and backward direction. If the horse is getting too close and in your space, put up your elbow or hand toward his face. Then, if he does not stop, jerk the lead lightly or firmly tap him on the nose to get his respect. Remember, you're the leader, not the horse. Be patient. It takes time to learn.

LIFE LESSON

God has chosen YOU. He has a special plan for your life and He wants to lead you into it. Every day, in things that happen to you, God uses those things to shape your life. Listen closely and find out what God wants you to learn.

Is he leading you, or do you try to go your own direction?

What challenges have I had today that God might be trying to teach a lesson that will help me in my future?

John 10:27   My sheep listen to my voice. I know them, and they follow me.

Psalms 37:23 The LORD makes secure the footsteps of the person who delights in him.

Day 8

- Submission

HORSE LESSON:

Will your horse lower his head for you? To get your horse to lower his head, you pull down pressure on the lead rope and hold. When he moves his head down, release the pressure. Repeat this until he is lowering his head. You can put your hand on top of his head and hold pressure until he responds and then release. If he is not responding to your hand, use the point of your finger putting pressure on the top of his head. Repeat this again and again to get it lower. It is important to release quickly when the horse lowers his head.

It is such a joy when you can lower your horse's head to put the bridle on or groom his ears. Horses are big and people are small, but God said for people to be in charge and have dominion over the animals.

LIFE LESSON:

Life is easier when we submit to God and draw near to Him. Let us tell our cares and problems to Him. He cares deeply for us.

Tell him some of your problems and things that bother you that you would like His help.

_____

_____

_____

_____

_____

_____

_____

_____

_____

I Peter 5:6-7 So make yourselves humble. Put yourselves under God's mighty hand. Then he will honor you at the right time. [7] Turn all your worries over to him. He cares about you.

James 4:6-8 But God continues to give us more grace. That's why Scripture says, "God opposes those who are proud. But he gives grace to those who are humble." [7] So obey God. Stand up to the devil. He will run away from you. [8] Come near to God, and he will come near to you. Wash your hands, you sinners. Make your hearts pure, you who can't make up your minds.

DAY 9

Grooming and looking good

HORSE LESSON:
Grooming your horse is an important time and opportunity for training. It is important to teach your horse to move from the pressure when you ask him to move his back or front quarters without going forward or backward--standing still while there is movement around him and moving out of your space when he is asked. Grooming is healthy for the skin and coat, and it feels good to the horse. It also helps to make the horse gentle and builds trust between you and the horse. If you are not in control on the ground, you will not be in control on his back. Use grooming as a time for training for the both of you.

LIFE LESSON:

As the comb and brush remove the tangles and dirt from the horse's hair and brings out the beauty of the horse, so does God's word bring out the beauty and glory of Christ in us.

Read some in your Bible in Proverbs and write about it below. How can His Word change you to show the beauty of Christ to others around you?

_____

_____

_____

_____

_____

_____

_____

_____

_____

_____

_____

Isaiah 61:3 He wants me to help those in Zion who are filled with sorrow. I will put beautiful crowns on their heads in place of ashes. I will anoint them with olive oil to give them joy instead of sorrow. I will give them a spirit of praise in place of a spirit of sadness. They will be like oak trees that are strong and straight. The LORD himself will plant them in the land. That will show how glorious he is.

Psalms 149:4 The LORD takes delight in his people. He awards with victory those who are humble.

DAY 10

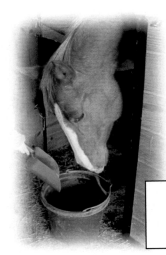

- Caring for your horse
- God loves you

HORSE LESSON:
Does your horse come running when you come with a bucket of feed?

When your horse learns what you have for him in the bucket and the care that you offer for his benefit, he will not forget. A horse that does not know may not trust you, and he will stand off until you show that you are not a threat to him. This is a time for patience to build trust. Some horses are not afraid and, at feed time, will push you around to get to the feed. To this horse, you need to establish respect and boundaries by applying pressure with a raised hand or a tap on the nose to move him out of your space until you allow him to come in.

Be very careful at feed time. Especially if there is more than one horse as they will often kick at each other and you can get caught in between them. This is why respect and boundaries are needed to keep you safe.

LIFE LESSON:

Psalms 23:1-7 says: The LORD is my shepherd. He gives me everything I need. ² He lets me lie down in fields of green grass. He leads me beside quiet waters. ³ He gives me new strength. He guides me in the right paths for the honor of his name. ⁴ Even though I walk through the darkest valley, I will not be afraid. You are with me. Your shepherd's rod and staff comfort me. ⁵ You prepare a feast for me right in front of my enemies. You pour oil on my head. My cup runs over. ⁶ I am sure that your goodness and love will follow me all the days of my life. And I will live in the house of the LORD forever.

Don't ever forget who loves and cares for you. The horse doesn't forget and neither should you.

Finding out what good things God has in store for you makes you want to come closer to him.

What are ways God cares for you? Write them below.

_____

_____

_____

_____

_____

_____

_____

Isaiah 1:3 The ox knows its master.
The donkey knows where its owner feeds it.
But Israel does not know me.
My people do not understand me."

Psalms 34:8 Taste and see that the Lord is good. Blessed is the person who goes to him for safety.

DAY 11

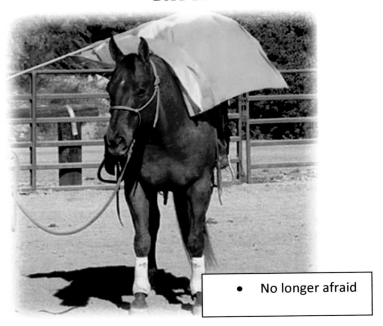

- No longer afraid

HORSE LESSON:

If you will desensitize your horse (free them from their fears), it will help prepare him for things he will encounter in the future. It will help make your riding experience better. Whether you are using a plastic bag, flag, or a rope, you want to start at a distance away and move closer as the horse accepts it. You want to be patient and reward him for his progress of not moving. Your goal is to teach your horse not to be afraid and to learn that these things that you are exposing him to will not harm him. It is very important to stop the threat when he accepts it. It is just as important that your horse knows that he can trust you.

LIFE LESSON:

Remember, God is preparing you today for the things you will face in the future. You can trust Him. He knows how frightened you are about things, and He wants you to be at peace. Do you have faith in Him enough to trust Him no matter what comes your way?

What are some of the things that frighten you?

_____

_____

_____

_____

_____

_____

_____

_____

_____

_____

I Corinthians 10:13 You are tempted in the same way all other human beings are. God is faithful. He will not let you be tempted any more than you can take. But when you are tempted, God will give you a way out. Then you will be able to deal with it.

Proverbs 3:5 Trust in the LORD with all your heart. Do not depend on your own understanding.

DAY 12

- Follow me

HORSE LESSON:
When your horse follows you, it shows that you have his attention and trust. Horses are "herd" animals, and they are all about following the leader. With your horse in the round pen and loose, drive him around with you in control of the direction and speed of the horse. When you take the pressure off and he stops, watch to see if he turns to face you. Reward with rest and turn and move away in another direction to see if he "hooks on" and follows you. When he looks away and doesn't follow, then drive him again controlling speed and direction. You need to be able to have him come to you and then send him away. Repeat over and over. Put pressure when he looks away, and release pressure when he looks at you when you stop. With your horse on a lead, lunge him and tug the lead and look at his hips. He should be facing you. Move his hips while he is still facing you. Leading your horse, he should stop when you stop and go when you go. Move away faster to create draw. Teaching a horse to follow teaches him to believe in you, trust and respect you.

LIFE LESSON:

Jesus is saying to all of us, "follow me".   Are you following Jesus? Is Jesus your leader? Are you hooked to Him? Does He have your full attention? Is it in Him that you trust and respect? What are some of the ways you are following Jesus?

_____

_____

_____

_____

_____

_____

Matthew 4:18-20 One day Jesus was walking beside the Sea of Galilee. There he saw two brothers, Simon Peter and his brother Andrew. They were throwing a net into the lake, because they were fishermen.
[19] "Come and follow me," Jesus said. "I will send you out to fish for people." [20] At once they left their nets and followed him.

Mark 8:34 Jesus called the crowd to him along with his disciples. He said, "Whoever wants to be my disciple must say no to themselves. They must pick up their cross and follow me.

DAY 13

Communication
• Learning the language

HORSE LESSON:

Do you speak the horse's language? If you teach your horse the English language and you do not learn horse language, then your horse will be smarter than you. (smile) He will most likely be the leader if that is the case. It is important that you learn to read and speak horse language. What I mean is that you learn to read his body language and you communicate to him with your body language. The first thing horses do when they meet each other is to establish who's the leader. To look at your horse is to put pressure and to look away is to release pressure. To raise your hand applies pressure and to lower your hand releases pressure. Watch horses interact with each other in the pasture and learn their language. This will help you to communicate to them in a way they understand and the way they do to each other.

LIFE LESSON:

Do you speak God's language? God knows and speaks all our languages. God's language is a spiritual language and a language of faith, truth, love, and life. Listen with your heart and watch for God's action around you. Read how God spoke with his children in the Bible and learn His language.

Can you recall some Bible characters and how God talked to them in a language they understood? It could have been He talked to their heart or mind. Maybe it was with nature. How has God talked to you?

_____

_____

_____

_____

_____

_____

Matthew 13:15 The hearts of these people have become stubborn.
  They can barely hear with their ears.
  They have closed their eyes.
Otherwise they might see with their eyes.
  They might hear with their ears.
  They might understand with their hearts.
They might turn to the Lord, and then he would heal them.'

Proverbs 15:31 Whoever listens to a warning that gives life will be at home among those who are wise.

DAY 14

- Standing tied

HORSE LESSON:

Safely tying your horse is important so that your horse will not be injured and that he will be there when you return after walking away. Tie your horse to something that is secure and that he will not break if he pulls. A post is the best because boards sometimes break or the nails pull loose from the pressure of a horse trying to get loose. When you tie your horse, do it in such a way that your horse can have his head level or slightly down in a relaxed position. Do not leave too much slack in the rope because it is possible the horse could get his foot caught in it. Before leaving your horse tied, be sure that he is standing relaxed. Always consider the dangers around where you are tying him. Sharp objects can harm your horse or your equipment because of noise and motion that might frighten your horse. Always use a knot that will have a quick release by pulling one end of the rope.

LIFE LESSON:
God places us at a "post", and when he returns, He wants to find us there. Are you where God placed you?

_____

_____

_____

_____

_____

_____

_____

_____

_____

_____

_____

Luke 19:30-31 "Go to the village ahead of you. As soon as you get there, you will find a donkey's colt tied up. No one has ever ridden it. Untie it and bring it here. [31] Someone may ask you, 'Why are you untying it?' If so, say, 'The Lord needs it.' "

DAY 15

- Loading for a trip

HORSE LESSON:

Can you load your horse in a trailer? Lead your horse to the trailer just as you would lead him to the barn. If there's a point where he stops and refuses to go any closer, turn and keep leading him in another direction. Keep making circles that brings him closer to the trailer. Make it work for him when moving away from the trailer but rest at the trailer. If he's curious about the trailer, let him look and smell. Let him take time to check it out. If he's not ready to get inside, move him away. Then begin again to move him closer. Repeat until he easily comes close to the trailer. When he begins to enter the trailer, keep pressure on him to encourage him to get inside. After he has gotten in, take the pressure off and reward his behavior. After a brief time, back him out and do the process over again until he is loading without any hesitation.

LIFE LESSON:

People are sometimes afraid to attend a church, much like a horse is afraid to go into a trailer. It may be that they have had a bad experience before or have been hurt. It could be that it is something strange and unknown to them. They are afraid. Nevertheless, when pressure of life on the outside is greater than the pressure on the inside, they enter and find rest and release from the pressures of the outside life.

Are you willing to load up and go where God wants to take you?

What things do you fear in life?

What door is God opening that He wants you to enter?

_____

_____

_____

_____

_____

_____

_____

_____

Exodus 33:14 The LORD replied, "I will go with you. And I will give you rest."

Psalms 4:8 In peace I will lie down and sleep. LORD, you alone keep me safe.

DAY 16

- Accepting new things
- Facing your fears

HORSE LESSON:
We ask a horse to accept things he is not used to. It is easy to be afraid of something that is new, different, or strange, and the same is true for a horse. He may want to jump and run from something of which he is unsure. This is when you must be the leader to introduce this strange object in a nonthreatening way so that the horse will understand that it will not harm him. This will require patience to allow the horse to look at, smell, and take some time before he is ok with the strange thing. As he takes his time evaluating the object, watch for the horse to relax. Some signs of relaxing is licking his lips, exhaling a big breath of air, or a slight change in his ears. It may require introducing him to the new and strange object several times with confidence, calmness, and patience. This will help the horse learn to cope and work things out.

LIFE LESSON:
God prepares us for our tomorrows by helping us through our trials and troubles today.

The fears you face, when conquered, builds confidence and makes you stronger. Experience will give you wisdom to face new things.

What are some things you've learned by experience?

_____

_____

_____

_____

_____

_____

_____

_____

_____

_____

_____

_____

I Peter 4:12 Dear friends, don't be surprised by the terrible things happening to you. The trouble you are having has come to test you. So don't feel as if something strange was happening to you.

James 1:3 Your faith will be tested. You know that when this happens it will produce in you the strength to continue.

DAY 17

- Expectation

HORSE LESSON:
What is your expectation of your horse today? Do you expect him to do tricks that he has not been taught? Do you expect him to perform in ways he has not been trained? Are you expecting him to be at a level where he has not been developed? Do not expect your horse to be any more than what he is right at this moment. That may be untrained and wild, or a beginner or an intermediately developed horse.

LIFE LESSON:

God does not expect us to be or do any more than we are capable of today. He knows our abilities and inabilities. God works with us to make us the best we can be. We may feel God is stretching us too far and it's too hard. But He is wise about developing us into more than we are today. Are you ready to be trained in God's school?

What are the lessons God is teaching you that challenge you?

_____

_____

_____

_____

_____

_____

_____

_____

_____

Hebrew 5:12 By this time you should be teachers. But in fact, you need someone to teach you all over again. You need even the simple truths of God's word. You need milk, not solid food. [13] Anyone who lives on milk is still a baby. That person does not want to learn about living a godly life. [14] Solid food is for those who are grown up. They have trained themselves to tell the difference between good and evil. That shows they have grown up themselves with a lot of practice. They can tell the difference between good and evil.

DAY 18

Foot Care

HORSE LESSON:

Will your horse give you his foot to pick it up to clean, check, or put on shoes? With a young horse especially, you want to start from the shoulder and rub down his leg on the outside. When he picks up his leg, remove your hand. Repeat this process over and over until the horse is relaxed and allows you to catch his foot. When you hold his foot, shake it up and down and then release it. This will help the horse to not feel restrained. You want him working with you, not fighting against you. Remember, be aware of the horse, and release the foot when you realize he is getting tired or anxious. You want the release of pressure to be on your terms. Reward good responses and discipline bad ones. Be patient. Patience makes a better trainer or horse person.

God wants the best for you!

LIFE LESSON:

It is important to be able to pick up your horse's foot without struggle…for the horse's safety and for yours. This takes a lot of trust. Likewise, it is very important that you are able to trust God and allow him to work in your life. God wants only the best for you. To pick up a horse's foot may seem unneeded to a horse until the day he picks up a stone and needs it removed. You want to be able to help him. The way God trains you may seem harsh or hard, but the day will come when you will see that what he has taught you was necessary. How is God teaching you to trust him?

_____

_____

_____

_____

_____

_____

_____

_____

Romans 8:37-39   No! In all these things we are more than winners! We owe it all to Christ, who has loved us. [38] I am absolutely sure that not even death or life can separate us from God's love. Not even angels or demons, the present or the future, or any powers can separate us. [39] Not even the highest places or the lowest, or anything else in all creation can separate us. Nothing at all can ever separate us from God's love. That's because of what Christ Jesus our Lord has done.

DAY 19

- Bridles and Bits
- Guidance

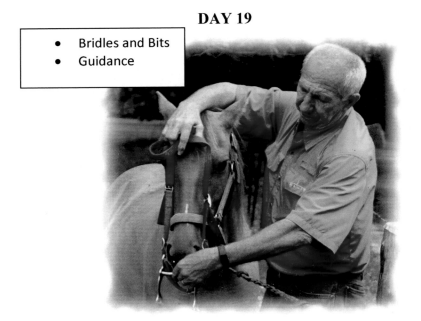

HORSE LESSON:

Put the bridle on your horse by first asking him to lower his head. Stand on the left side of your horse. Hold the bridle at the top in your right hand, and with your left hand, hold the bit to the horse's lips. With your thumb, encourage the horse to open his mouth. When he opens his mouth, pull up the bridle with the right hand. Be gentle, and don't hit his teeth with the bit. Always reward your horse for responding in the correct way. Rub their neck or nose.

To remove the bridle, take hold of the top of the bridle and pull it off from the horse's ears and the let the bridle down. Wait for the horse to open his mouth and let the bit out. With patience, the horse will learn that a bit in his mouth is not such a bad thing.

LIFE LESSON:

The Word of God is like a bridle to us. It is not a bad thing to have in our hearts and mind, for by it we are guided in the right paths.

Scriptures not only tell us what NOT to do, but also things we should be doing. Can you name of few of each of these? Write them below.

_____

_____

_____

_____

_____

_____

_____

_____

_____

_____

Psalms 119:105   Your word is like a lamp that shows me the way. It is like a light that guides me.

Psalms 48:14   This God is our God for ever and ever. He will be our guide to the very end.

James 3:3   We put a small piece of metal in the mouth of a horse to make it obey us. We can control the whole animal with it.

DAY 20

- Saddle up your horses

HORSE LESSON:

A cowboy will say to a horse, "Will you carry my saddle? If you will carry my saddle, you can wear my brand." (He means he will take care of him.) The purpose of the horse is to carry the saddle or pull the wagon, to plow the field, or some other task. Doing these things is not what comes natural to the horse, but it is service that he learns.

When saddling a horse, first introduce him to the saddle pad. Let him see it and smell it, and then touch it to his shoulder, and then slide it on his back into the right place just above his withers with the front of it. Introduce the saddle the same way as you did the pad. If he moves away, repeat the process, moving slowly and with patience. You want your horse to receive the saddle. You are not forcing it on him. The girth under this stomach may feel strange to him. A way to prepare the horse for this is to rub his belly when you are grooming him. When you pull the cinch, don't over-tighten. Move the horse around some and then re-tighten it.

LIFE LESSON

We all have a purpose in life. You are given various gifts and abilities that God will ask you to use for Him. God will be gentle as He teaches you to trust him as he 'lays' these gifts on you. Someday, it will seem natural to use your gifts for Christ, as it will be for the horse to carry the saddle.

What abilities and talents is God giving you? If you know, write them down. If not, ask God what you can do for Him.

_____

_____

_____

_____

_____

Luke 14:27 Whoever doesn't carry their cross and follow me can't be my disciple.

Matthew 11:29-30 Become my servants and learn from me. I am gentle and free of pride. You will find rest for your souls. [30] Serving me is easy, and my load is light."

DAY 21

REINING:
- Guiding a horse
- Guided by God

HORSE LESSON:

Will your horse stop when you pull on the reins? Will he turn when you pull to the right or left? He does not stop only because you pull but because you release. Pulling on both the reins is a signal to stop but release is the reward. The horse is seeking the release of pressure. When you pull one rein, he is signaled to turn, and as he turns, the pressure is released. It took me a long time to learn that, and now I know why my horse would keep running. When he stopped, I would still be pulling back! So why stop if the pressure is not released.

LIFE LESSON:

When God wants you to stop something, or if he wants you to do something special like speak to another person that might look lonely, or take up for someone that others are bothering, he sends little signals. To me, it might be a "feeling" that I should do it.

What things do you think God does to guide you if he wants you to do something?

_____

_____

_____

_____

_____

I have learned that if I respond to the signal of God that I will find the release of pressure. What a reward!

> *I Samuel 15:22* "…What pleases the LORD more?
>   Burnt offerings and sacrifices, or obeying the LORD?
> It is better to obey than to offer a sacrifice.
>   It is better to do what he says than to offer the fat of rams.

DAY 22

- Ground driving

HORSE LESSON:

Ground driving a horse is a good way to find out how well he will respond to the reins to turn right or left and how well he will stop. Ground driving is also a good way to teach a young horse how to rein. In a round pen, after your horse knows how to lunge, you can take two lunge lines attached to the bit on each side and run those lines through the stirrups on the saddle. While standing in position for lunging your horse, you can begin asking him to move. Standing slightly to the center, move your horse around you. As he goes to your left, you can turn him to the right. As he goes to your right, you can turn him left. Standing at a safe distance directly behind him, you can drive him forward then stop him by pulling on the lines. Be sure to release the pressure as soon as he stops, but apply pressure if he moves before you ask. Reward correct responses generously, and remember that standing directly behind the horse may sometimes be out of his sight. He is listening and learning to trust your interaction.

LIFE LESSON:

Are you learning to respond to God's direction for your life when God tugs on you? Can you feel or hear Him guiding you even when you cannot see Him?

Write your thoughts on today's devotion.

_____

_____

_____

_____

_____

_____

_____

Psalms 32:8 I will guide you and teach you the way you should go. I will give you good advice and watch over you with love.

Isiah 30:21 You will hear your Teacher's voice behind you. You will hear it whether you turn to the right or the left. It will say, "Here is the path I want you to take. So walk on it."

John 16:13 But when the Spirit of truth comes, he will guide you into all the truth. He will not speak on his own. He will speak only what he hears. And he will tell you what is still going to happen.

DAY 23

Getting on your horse
- The journey

HORSE LESSON:

It is time to get on your horse and ride. Stand near the left side of the horse, up close to his shoulder. You want to pull your horse's nose into you just a little bit, so if he moves, it will be towards you and not away. Put your left foot in the stirrup while holding the reins and saddle horn, then spring up and stand with your hips twisted so that you are facing toward the horse's head. If the horse stands and is calm, you are ready to slide your right leg across his back. Let your horse relax, and if this is the first time for the horse, get back off and reward his good behavior. Remember, in the horse's world, only enemies try to jump on their backs. This is not natural to the horse, and he must learn to trust you. Repeat getting on the horse from both sides until he stands calm and relaxed.

Now, you are ready to ask him to move forward. It helps by pulling one rein to ask him to step to the side. Just a few steps at a time, and then slowly continue to walk and stop at your command. You want be able to "whoa" as well as "go". This is the beginning of a wonderful journey with your horse.

LIFE LESSON:
Your journey with Christ will be a wonderful journey also. Trust will be built as you continue to read His word and talk to Him in your prayers. God will be patient with you. Be patient in your response to Him also. You will soon find He is the best friend you ever had. He cares for you and together you can change your world.

Write and tell Him how much this journey means to you.

_____

_____

_____

_____

_____

Amos 3:3 Do two people walk together unless they've agreed to do so?

Psalms 48:14 This God is our God for ever and ever. He will be our guide to the very end.

DAY 24

Flexing
- Bending not breaking

HORSE LESSON:

Flexing your horse is a good training for young or old horses. You flex your horse by pulling on the rein to move his head to the right or left. It teaches them to be soft to the pull on the reins. This is something you can do standing on the ground before you even get on. Bring his nose around toward you, and when he gives to the pressure, then release. You will want to do this on both sides many times. If you can control his head, you can control his body. This is very important when you are riding. The softer the touch, the more enjoyable it makes the experience of riding. After you have gotten on your horse and before you move, you can flex your horse. Make it a pleasant experience for him. You pull and he moves his head and gives you his nose. It is good when he is flexing even to the point of where he touches your leg with his nose as you sit in the saddle. A little goes a long way.

LIFE LESSON:

How good are you at flexing? When God pulls softly on your reins, do you give Him your head and heart and will? It makes for a more enjoyable life when we do. What ways can you give more of your head, heart, and will to God?

_____

_____

_____

_____

_____

_____

_____

Romans 6:13 Don't give any part of yourself to serve sin. Don't let any part of yourself be used to do evil. Instead, give yourselves to God. You have been brought from death to life. So give every part of yourself to God to do what is right.

Romans 12:1 Brothers and sisters, God has shown you his mercy. So I am asking you to offer up your bodies to him while you are still alive. Your bodies are a holy sacrifice that is pleasing to God. When you offer your bodies to God, you are worshiping him in the right way. ^{2} Don't live the way this world lives. Let your way of thinking be completely changed. Then you will be able to test what God wants for you. And you will agree that what he wants is right. His plan is good and pleasing and perfect.

DAY 25

- **Stepping back**

HORSE LESSON:

Now your horse will move to the right or left and forward, but what about backing? While you are still on the ground, it is a good time to start training your horse to back up. Standing in front of your horse, a little to the side, put pressure on the halter pushing his head down and back. Hold that pressure until he moves one foot backward and then release. Reward his obedience. If he doesn't move with pressure on the nose, push on his shoulder and release pressure when he moves only one foot. Continue this training process until he is moving with as little pressure as possible.

A good thing to do when you first get on your horse is to take a few steps back before going forward. To teach your horse to back up when you are in the saddle, you need to pull the reins and hold the pressure until he moves backward. Be patient and reward for the slightest move. Continue this training process, and over time, he will be moving back at your command.

LIFE LESSON:
God once asked the sun to go backward.

God asked the sea to go back.

It may seem really hard to step back when we want to rush ahead. But listening and responding to God's command is for our good. He sometimes asks us to step back to allow another to go ahead. But remember, He said that the last shall be first and the first shall be last.

When was a time God asked you to step back? Write about it.

_____

_____

_____

_____

_____

II Kings 20:10 It's easy for the shadow to go forward ten steps," said Hezekiah. "So have it go back ten steps."

Exodus 14:21 Then Moses reached out his hand over the Red Sea. All that night the LORD pushed the sea back with a strong east wind. He turned the sea into dry land. The waters were divided.

DAY 26

- Riding and living in balance

HORSE LESSON:
When you ride, do you ride balanced? What is your posture? When you are riding a horse, your shoulders should be back with your back straight, knees bent with your toes turned up, and your heels down. Your feet should be slightly forward with yours hands in line with your feet. When your horse stops, you should sit deeper into the saddle and, when he moves forward, you should move slightly upward. As your horse turns right or left, you should turn your body with him. Always look in the direction you are going, and this will help your body to be in the right position and balanced. When going downhill, lean a little back with feet slightly forward. When going uphill, lean a little forward with feet slightly back. You are actually staying level with the ground, and the horse is angling down or up with the features of the ground.

LIFE LESSON:

A very important question to ask yourself is, "Am I living my life with balance or is my life and thinking out of balance?"

In Daniel, 5:27, Belshazzer, the king, was told, "**…you have been weighed on scales. And you haven't measured up to God's standard.**" His life was out of balance.

A very important question to ask yourself is, "Am I living my life with balance?" Write your thoughts.

_____

_____

_____

_____

_____

_____

_____

_____

Ecclesiastes 3:17 I said to myself, "God will judge godly and sinful people alike.
He has a time for every act.
He has a time to judge everything that is done."

DAY 27

- Standing still

HORSE LESSON:

When you stop your horse, do you put him in the "neutral" gear or in "park"? In neutral, he may go wherever he wants, but in park, he stands still. If you want to take a picture from a horse's back while you are in the saddle, you need him in "park". To be able to look at a map of the trail you are riding, you also need him in "park". How do you teach him to park? First, ride him enough until he desires park. (smile) Then stop him, relax, and release pressure. Reward him for the stop. If he moves, correct him, and if he still moves, then make it your idea and make him move more. Continue this process and soon he will learn that park means "rest" and to move means "back to work".

LIFE LESSON:

How good are you in staying in park when God places you somewhere? Do you get anxious and want to move? When something is threatening, do you run away?

There are times that God puts us in park to teach us a lesson. Other times, it is to protect us from some unknown danger. Learn to listen to God about when and where to move.

Has God asked you to stop and be still before? Why would or why did he do that? Can you recall a time?

_____

_____

_____

_____

_____

_____

Exodus 14:13-14 Moses answered the people. He said, "Don't be afraid. Stand firm. You will see how the LORD will save you today. Do you see those Egyptians? You will never see them again. [14] The LORD will fight for you. Just be still."

Isiah 41:10 So do not be afraid. I am with you.
   Do not be terrified. I am your God.
I will make you strong and help you.
   I will hold you safe in my hands.
   I always do what is right

DAY 28

- Staying safe

HORSE LESSON:
One of the most dangerous times around a horse is when you come into a pen with feed and there are other horses around. It is difficult to watch all the horses as they may surround you, and at the same time, trying to get away from a bite or kick from another horse. It makes you vulnerable to a 'run-over' or a kick that is meant for another horse. It is better when you can place feed in their feeding containers before you call the horses, or place the containers where you can put the feed in from over the fence. Placing the horses in separate stalls is even safer. If you have to enter the pen with multiple horses, carry a whip or flag that will allow you to have an extension of your arm to be able to keep the horses out of your space. The horses must respect you and your space. When eating is on their mind, it can be difficult. A good training is to have a halter and lead on your horse and give him food. Then take him away and require him to give you his full attention before allowing him to return to the food. Allow him then to eat without putting pressure on him. Help him to relax and know that you are not a challenge to his food.

LIFE LESSON:
Do you feel that God is keeping you from what you want and may be hungry for...from what you desire? Give God your full attention and follow where He leads. You will find that He will give you more than you can imagine.

What do you desire most in life?

_____

_____

_____

_____

_____

_____

_____

_____

_____

_____

_____

Psalms 23:1 The LORD is my shepherd. He gives me everything I need.

Matthew 6:26 Look at the birds of the air. They don't plant or gather crops. They don't put away crops in storerooms. But your Father who is in heaven feeds them. Aren't you worth much more than they are?

DAY 29

- Leaving the round pen

HORSE LESSON:

Now you are coming outside to trail ride with others and their horses…horses that you do not know their habits or training. Horses, if they are not controlled by their riders, will go about establishing leadership. They will threaten with their ears laid back and turning their head to challenge another horse that is getting too close. When riding with others, you need to not only watch your horse but also the horses around you. You need to read what the horses are saying. The kick or bite may be meant for your horse or another's horse, but it is very easy for you to be hit or bit. Watch your horse and make sure that he is paying attention to you and not threatening to the other horses. Watch not to follow too closely behind another horse. When passing, do not linger at the rear of another horse and make sure that the other person knows that you are coming up beside. When you stop and tie up for a rest, remember to give enough space between horses so they are not fighting with others.

LIFE LESSON:

Do you sometimes feel that God has placed you with others that are hard to get along with? Remember to give them some space and life will be much easier. Do not challenge them for the lead or control. When it is time for you to move ahead, do it quickly, not allowing them time to strike at you.

Write your thoughts about the devotion today.

_____

_____

_____

_____

_____

_____

_____

_____

_____

Amos 3:3 Do two people walk together unless they've agreed to do so?

I Corinthians 14:33 God is not a God of disorder. He is a God of peace, just as in all the churches of the Lord's people.

DAY 30

- Returning your horse to his home (pasture or stall)
- Watching for our own safety with horses and in life

LESSON:

After working with your horse, it's time to turn him back into the pasture or stall. How do you safely do this without being in danger of being kicked? Many times after you've worked your horse, he's ready to kick up his heels and run in the pasture to see his friends. If you lead him to the gate and stand beside him to take off his halter, there's a possibility that he could kick as he runs by. He's not trying to hurt you, but it's a common thing that horses do sometimes. The safe thing to do is to lead your horse into the pasture and have him turn around and face you to remove the halter. The direction he's going to go is away from you instead of going by you. You can watch him more closely. When putting your horse in a stall, stand by the door outside and have your horse go in and turn around facing you to remove the halter or lead. Being safe and having a good experience makes you look forward to returning to have interaction with your horse.

LIFE LESSION:

The Lord cares about your safety. He is watching over you to keep you from harm. Sometimes, we put ourselves into harm's way. He wants us to be wise and to watch. Be aware of others that you are in close contact with and the dangers that someone might bring to you. What are some areas in your life where you need God to watch over you?

_____

_____

_____

_____

_____

_____

_____

_____

_____

_____

_____

_____

_____

*Genesis 28:15 "*I am with you. I will watch over you everywhere you go. And I will bring you back to this land. I will not leave you until I have done what I have promised you."

Sam and Ann Phillips

CONCLUSION

I want to thank you for reading these devotions for Thirty Days of Round Pen Training. I do not claim to know everything about horse training or about God. I am still learning and will be for the rest of my life. For both you and your horse, it is a lifetime of training. They say that if you do something for thirty days, a habit will be established. It is my desire and prayer that you will develop good habits of learning and knowing God every day and will continue to learn and give good leadership to your horse.

Happy Trails!!!

Sam & Ann Phillips

Sam and Ann Phillips

If you have enjoyed these devotions, please leave a "review" on Amazon and other book sites so someone can find the book.

Thank you.

Sam & Ann Phillips

Sam and Ann Phillips

Made in the USA
Lexington, KY
05 October 2017